Beneath the Rime

Also by Siriol Troup:

Drowning up the Blue End

SIRIOL TROUP

Beneath the Rime

Shearsman Books
Exeter

First published in the United Kingdom in 2009 by
Shearsman Books Ltd
58 Velwell Road
Exeter EX4 4LD

www.shearsman.com

ISBN   978-1-84861-030-9

Cover image:
Winter Sun by Renée Deschamps.
Copyright © Renée Deschamps, 2006.

Contents

for my parents

*Die Gedanken
machen das Wasser eisig.
(Thoughts
make the water icy.)*

Günter Eich

THE HUMAN POSITION

BEGINNINGS

See the man with the goose
on his head—that's Negneg
the Great Cackler
trumpeting wake-up calls
to the protoplasm,
his honking cry
the *souffle prophétique*
that fanned creation.
That egg in his hand
is worth two bushy
phoenixes: the sun's inside,
a dazzling yolk
in clouds of albumen.

Don't let him crack you up
with his small pink bill
and chestnut spectacles—
the world's at stake:
a shudder on the horizon.

FAUN

L'après-midi d'un faune, Nijinsky
for Alison and Stephen Musgrave

When he comes to the edge to drink
you recognize his angular grace—
slim hips, hair quiffed into horns,
thumb cocked like a gun.

You know him from disco nights
and back-seat sex,
hot tongue on your pale skin,
that dreamy look that tells you he's high

on something you've never tried:
the power to take on other forms,
to find what remains in him
of the animal or the pagan.

Goatish in hooves and fur,
then suddenly drawing music
from a reed or a bone
as if the world's a shadow on stone

and all that matters
is the sound of the pipe,
the play of sunlight on water,
the abstract beauty of limbs.

NOX ELEPHANTORUM

—Elephant Night at the Coliseum

Climb the railings by moonlight—you'll find us
on our knees in the ring, turning tricks
under the sky's black awning. Such eloquent
desolation: the rime of ivory on tufa,
a breeze down the stairwells, the whiff
of dung and *pozzolana*. We have only
a few hours each night, but they are very long.

How shall we entertain you? Walk the tightrope
backwards? Toss stray cats in the air, watch them
break as they fall? For Germanicus
we danced the graveyard shuffle, our big feet
tender as pincushions, a crimson ellipsis
on the sand. The people roared, the vultures
lunged and hissed over the bleachers.

Let me be your guide. Once there were
statues, frescoes, trapdoors, marble seats, sails
flying through cloud. The butchery defied
imagination: bulls, bears, crocodiles,
tigers and giraffes—an alphabet of beasts
slaughtered *ad libitum*, carousels
of blood. Listen, you can hear the skirl

of tusks along the colonnades.
I had a mother once. These ears are for
remembering: the feverish sea, psoriasis
of salt on skin, the subterranean
cells, the bite of chains. Now, in the centre
of the herd, we place the ones who cannot
die, shading them with the bark of our hides,

with memories of acacias rooted in heat-haze.
They weep like rocks, piteously, below
the range of human hearing. In summer
the moths come, creamy as baobab flowers,
wings like gauze on their wounds. How many
of us lie buried in this vanished world?
Step closer, let me show you the little paths

that wind among the ruins. The travertine vaults.
The drains gathering water from the hills of Rome.
The Vestals sat here. Here's the spot where tongues
of lightning set fire to the upper floors. Here
twenty elephants were killed, but not before
we'd raised our trunks to heaven, causing the crowd
to rain down curses on Pompey. And here

you stand with your guidebook, staring at things
you cannot see. Soon it will be dawn.
You'll leave with our dust on your feet, our breath
on your neck, our tears on your dry cheeks.
Will you remember how we died? How little
we asked of the gods? How the moon tonight
was encompassed by a light unknown in your land?

ABOUT SUFFERING
Two Photographs of W. H. Auden

How well the camera understands
the human position, giving us the same scene
in both shots—a café in Venice,
a table, a tray, two glasses of wine.

Three of them in the first photograph—
Day Lewis and Spender buttoned up
while Wystan holds forth in the corner,
jabbing his finger like a thin cigar.

In the second, Chester Kallman
sits beside him, open-necked and tanned,
eyes turned away towards the lens,
oblivious of his lover's loving gaze.
The others have gone, the glasses
are almost empty, but the sun still shines
as it has to on the white legs disappearing
under the table, and Wystan, who has always known
that suffering takes place
while someone else is flirting or smoking a cigarette or just
          idly watching
the miraculous behinds of sailors strutting their stuff in the square,
must go on smiling, must go on
telling some amazing story
as the camera flashes, and his tears fall down.

THE PENANCE OF ST JOHN CHRYSOSTOM
After Lucas Cranach

He wanted the simple life:
a roof of rock, birdsong to wake him up,
cupped hands for berries, water, prayer.
But there was always that graphic primal urge—
the roebuck's horns, the needle-lust
of larch and spruce and pine,
church-steeples throbbing in his mind.

When he found her in the mouth of his cave
he waxed like a candle. Now he's on his knees
and when their child looks round or calls his name,
he's just part of the landscape:
a scar of schist where horsetails sprout like hair,
his fingers rooting in the ground,
his penance hardening into stone.

KNOWLEDGE

She wanted the world—
he closed his eyes to shut it out,
threw her an apple:
Take that!

She bit her lip
and knowledge flowed
like blood.

It tasted good,
she discovered,
saucing his rib.

COUNTRY LIVING

Monday to Friday we're alone with the rabbits,
Madame and I. Up at dawn with the smell
of wet straw and piss-a-bed, the piebald does
spaced out on ammonia behind the wire.

I slip the bolts, hear them jolt as I enter,
a skitter of hearts and toenails, whiskery hysterics.
Madame smacks my wrist: speak to them gently,
reward them when they come.

She calls them each by name, nuzzles and smooches,
nibbles their loose fur, their dippy tails—
mes biches, mes pucelles, mes allumeuses.
I clean their water-bowls and disinfect their beds.

On Sunday, she blocks her ears and weeps
into the casserole. Monsieur lays down his fork
and strokes her hand, then tucks in with relish,
slurping the thick juice until it trickles down his chin.

Pauvre Geneviève!
I take the afternoon off, light a candle
to St. Gertrude, let a boy in the market-place
stick his fist up my skirt.

The night I leave, I fill the bowls with foxgloves,
ivy, corn-lilies, creeping butterweed.
Push my fingers through the mesh.
Watch them come to me like whores.

Black Pudding

I miss the last bus home and walk the rest,
past the south tower where the moonlit
jaquemart hammers his bell and a hundred white
pigeons ruffle the square like ghosts.

Lights on in the kitchen—Monsieur in red
pyjamas chopping parsley and sage
with his scimitar. Through the glass I catch
the opal eye of a hog's head

turning deaf ears to *'La Vie en Rose'*
as heart and lungs plunge into the mincer.
Leeks, onions, wild savory, a litre
of purple blood: he licks the juice,

inflates the tube of gut, then stuffs
the meat in like a foot in a sock, hitches
the knots, holds out the string of sausages
and sings *"c'est lui pour moi"* in his rough

baritone. When I creep in, he primes
his greasy lips and smears my cheeks *comme ci
comme ça*. The room smells of death, racey
and sweet, and as he takes me in his arms,

je sens en moi mon coeur qui bat . . .

LES MOTS JUSTES

His text is dense. All afternoon
we tease out pith and gist, my notebook
charged with possibilities. I ache
to bridge the chasm between tongues.

By midnight I'm ready for bed.
He shuffles sheets, accuses my version
of being too faithful, a rigid imitation
of the source. 'Use your heart not your head,'

he urges. 'Forget *les mots justes*—
let the meaning quicken in your loins.'
He shuts my dictionary, tears up my list
of synonyms. I read between his lines.

HARVESTING

Because I'm ignorant, he takes me to the fields,
plants me between the rows, fills my cupped
hands with grasses, shows me how to blow and rub
until the chaff floats free like a cloud of peeled

insect wings, pale and papery in the blue dusk.
I swirl the grains in my palm, groats and kernels
furled tight as nuts, a hive of weevils
glazed and vulnerable without their husks,

swarming like light. Touching them one by one
he points out nuggets of yellow wheat, pearls
of barley, grey oats muzzled like cowrie shells,
rye seeds smooth as Chinese celadon—

'du blé, de l'orge, de l'avoine et du seigle'—
all gone in a puff as the wind from his lips
whistles over my wrist and my arm to the nape
of my neck and the long ear of my spine.

Willow Pattern

Each afternoon he walks me ragged,
paths dusty with catkins, fleshy
and sulphurous, a tapenade of grief.

It's the same old story:
towers and crooked fences,
a waiting boat, *le pont des suicides*.
Even the birds are dropping.

We begin where we end.
These trees with their blue leaves
have survived beyond imagining.

SIXPENCES

Only a child, but not too young to know
about belonging: so already it was
a kind of betrayal—the empty room,
the winter sun discovering the jar
on the shelf, the rapturous clink and
chink of metal against glass.

They gushed in her lap, easier than water
from a jug, a stream of silver sweet as
a dowry, too many to count aloud or
in her head, each one so thin
it seemed an optical illusion—
a flash of light, a weathered palm.

She filled her pockets, felt the tug and
lilt as she moved, a pleasure so secret
no one had told her its name: not greed, not
envy—and the theft not a theft at all, unless
feelings could somehow be stolen,
speckled eggs from a high nest.

How her fingertips ran through their promises!
Steeped in Coca-Cola, they came up bright
as blades, too precious for spending and soon
to go out of circulation anyway,
translated from legal tender
into the currency of dreams.

THE CRYPTOGRAM
after David Mamet

Off-stage is where it's happening.
A blanket tears, a teapot crashes to the floor.
Shoes are taken off and packed.
Rooms give up their secrets in a hotel corridor.
A book is borrowed and the wrong one given back.

What do they mean, those spectral stairs
that lead to heaven?
Can you smell your childhood at the top?
They've boxed it up like junk—
you'll need a knife to cut the twine.

Downstairs everything's hunky-dory:
cool surfaces and fifties curves,
sleek hair, a skirt smoothed down,
the rug just so, the cushions geometric.
The plant on the sideboard
may or may not be plastic.

It's like moving in with Edward Hopper—
everyone staying up late,
whisky glowing in the tumblers,
each object given an edge by artificial light—

and for a few moments
happiness is still possible.
Socks will protect bare feet.
Needle and thread will mend a blanket.
A warm lap will help you fall asleep.

If only the tea hadn't spilt—
What? Did I what? What? I've spilt the tea.

If only you knew
who made the tear,
who snapped the photograph,
who bought and sold the knife,
who went on the camping-trip.

If only you hadn't—

They're going to pieces,
shooting off words like guns,
rattling the cups on the tray,
bringing the house down.

If only you hadn't seen—

The rug's rolled up,
the furniture removed,
lampshades doffed like hats.

If only you hadn't—

Too late to sleep now. Too late for
shoes photographs books knives.
Things occur in our lives,
the meaning of them is not clear.

Too late to sleep now
in your tent under the stars.
The cipher's found,
the knife's in your hand,
and you've already started
up the stairs.

On the Rocks

Three of us there that day, two nudists laid out
like mackerel fillets on a slab, their state
of nature making a fool of me as I cursed the wind
in anorak and trainers. *We are the guardians
of this beach,* their bodies cried, so I left them
keeping faith with the earth. From a distance
their smiles were smug, their limbs refined
and gleaming, then suddenly storm clouds slammed
in from the sea, skuas began to scream, and I thought
someone should tell them to get dressed. I zipped
my fleece, noticing—as I ran—two small dead
puffins on the rocks, their bright beaks chinked
like cups, and all around, the sand as sharp
as chopped-up fingernails varnished a shocking pink.

FLOE

Our tracks once told us where we were.
We'd crack the whip and grip
the horse's flanks, certain we'd reach
the lake in time to catch the boat
to take us to the other side.

Now, mile after mile, snow scrolls
into the night. The world's reduced
to white-out: heartbeats and hoofprints,
a jangle of frost on iron, skeins
of snowgeese cutting up the sky.

We ride and ride—sweat pours,
the road goes on and on and on.
When we stop at the first lights
to ask a local girl how far
there's still to go, she stares

as if we've missed the plot,
then points to the black water just
behind. 'Didn't you come by boat?'
We turn towards the frozen sheet
that bore our weight across

without our knowledge,
and those cold fingers we now see
lurking beneath the rime
rise up to seize our reins
and smash our own thin ice.

DETACHMENT

He remembers the day, not the country,
one landscape much like another
after the war, glimpsed from a moving truck.
A village station, its name long gone,
though he can still recall the orchard
neglected beyond the platform, the sun
shivering through nettles, the dewpond
silvered by mist. He had his orders:
set up a rest-place for the army heading north,
a chance for tired men to eat and drink,
wash and smoke and take a piss.
He briefed his soldiers: bricks and planks
for tables, pews from the nearby church.

He didn't ask where they'd come from
or what they'd seen. He watched them
eat their rations beside the empty train
then spread out through the trees, squatting
in the long grass, moving their bowels
among the cratered fruit, stooping
at washstands propped beside the tracks
to dip their hands in German helmets
filled with soapy water.

SNOW IN APRIL

And what if this were the last snow ever, this white dream
dropping from the sky in British Summer Time—
freak April flurries that fool the leafing trees,
the unsuspecting garden chairs?

Would you rush out to capture muffled streets
and feathered lawns, soft-topped cars, fresh-iced
gingerbread houses, cast your fallen angels
on a pristine continent, try to take in once and for all

the miracle of snowflakes tenderly reforming your world
so years from now there'll be a softness to fall back on
when, lifting your head from the page, you catch

the whitebeam's melting buds beyond the pane
and with a shivered spine, a chill on your tongue,
finally understand you won't see snow again.

THE FINAL STRETCH

*Having used dogs to haul their sledges over the pack ice towards
the North Pole, Fridtjof Nansen and Hjalmar Johansen finally
reached open water on August 6th 1895, with only two dogs left.*

Lift your head from the snow, Kaifas,
this is the final stretch. One hundred
and forty-six days, over six hundred
miles on the ice. Tomorrow
at the glacier's edge there will be open
water and the plash of little waves
against canvas. The sledges will fall
silent, the kayaks will dance like Samoyeds.

Bear blood on the wind, a wounded
bear-cub lowing in the distance, no cartridge
to spare for his pain. His wails track us
across the floe, a bitter requiem
for the fresh meat in our gut. Do you
remember, Kaifas, how this journey
began? The market at Berezov,
the stink of reindeer skins and brandy,

the Ostiaks in their reincalf caps
bartering for dogs? How far we have come
since then, following the twisted line
of lichen across the Urals
to the frozen lanes of this white world.
Forty we were at the beginning,
beautiful dogs, thick coats, pricked ears, bright
eyes, ready for anything. Now we are two,

Kaifas and Suggen, high-priest and thug,
waiting under the dark water-sky
while our masters wave their hats and celebrate

with chocolate. So many deaths, and I
have watched them all: the ones I barely knew
who strangled on their ropes; my brother
Gammelen taken by a bear; poor Job, poor
Fox, torn into pieces by the other dogs,

Livjaegeren felled by Johansen's spear,
his skinned flesh thrown to us for supper;
Katta, Kvik, Baro, Klapperslangen,
Potifar . . . I have sat by their corpses
and waited for their souls to fly up
from this hostile land towards the forests
of Siberia where the earth is soft
and wolves howl louder than the Arctic wind.

Now we have served our purpose. See, Kaifas,
how the sky fills with birds—little auks,
skuas, kittiwakes, fulmars, ivory gulls,
terns tacking through the mist like prayers.
Bear-breath puckers the snow-drifts, the air
is brackish with seal-fume. We face
each other's masters, they cannot face
their own. Two shots—two easy deaths—

but who will watch our corpses on this last
sheet of floating ice while they set off
in their swift kayaks, paddling towards the land?

LUNCH AT THE DACHAU CAFÉ

i Car Park

The car park's overflowing
but still we come, bumper
to bumper through the trees.

The land's been cleared for us,
alders and birches lying down
for coaches, buses, dormobiles.

They've dug in gravel,
planted clumps of grass,
but damp red earth wells up

under our wheels, sticks
to our shoes, stays with us
when we leave.

ii Poplars

They mark the Lagerstrasse
where the barracks stood,
two rows of poplars on the road to hell.

A photograph from 1938
shows spindly nursery trees,
their shadows thinner than a man's.

By April '45 they've soared
and spread, their spires
already jabbing at the clouds.

They've seen the century out
but won't survive much longer,
short-lived cultivars

plagued by disease,
at best one of a crowd, a screen
providing shelter from the wind.

Cut down
they'll go on sprouting
underground, sending out

runners from their roots,
new stems, new shoots to raise
a monument of bark,

a choir of leaves.

iii *Lockers*

How familiar it smells, this room full of *Spinde*—
a locker-room at school, the wood scrubbed white
before the start of term.

But here the punishments doled out
for scuffs and stains are
unimaginable,

the only subject taught
a language easy to get the hang of:
what the dogs say when they bark.

iv *Floors*

The floors are planks of pine
but shine like burnished oak
or hardwoods from Brazil
imported in the nineteenth century
to deck the rooms of Ludwig's
palaces: cedar, mahogany,
lace-wood and lemon-wood.

They reek of linseed oil,
fresh beeswax, turpentine,
though all the prisoners had
was elbow grease that leaked
like fear into the common grain,
staining the knots and whorls
a reddish brown.

v *What chilled my spine at Dachau*

wasn't the hollow motto on the gate,
the silent showers, the reconstructed huts,
the bunker cells or crematorium

but photographs of dogs as plump as sin,
boxers and labradors that sprawled
on polished boards like landed whales

or waddled through the camp on beefy limbs,
their rippled flesh so satisfied and sleek
I threw up images of all those hands

that held their leads and tossed them meat and bones
and stroked their ears and wiped their muddy paws
and patted them, then loaded up the guns.

vi **Lunch at the Dachau Café**

we palm the squares of chocolate which we've had for weeks
bought at the station kiosk for a rainy day
suck them in secret as we read a sign
that tells us next year when we come there'll finally be a
café at Dachau where we'll eat our lunch a
café at Dachau where the staff will look us in the eye and
    know
we're clutching our thighs hugging our sweet rolls of flesh
piling our plates eating oh eating for comfort

PROVINCIAL

> *'Dachau is a picturesque provincial town . . . the Schlosscafé serves*
> *excellent cakes'*
>
> *(The Rough Guide to Germany)*

This town without a twin is a ghost town sidelined
from the main event: car park empty, supermarkets closed.
We're the only visitors from out of town.
No trace of the annual *Volksfest* in the tidy streets.
The locals are eating lunch inside, keeping themselves
to themselves as they have always done.

In the castle café, waitresses in dirndls bring us coffee and cakes.
A wall-eyed man addresses portraits of Wittelsbachs.
Poplars are whispering *complicit, complicit, complicit . . .*
Roses are heavy with buds.

This could be ours,
this could be anywhere on earth,
this picturesque provincial town so quietly insisting
nothing happens here.

A Small Adjustment

HIROHITO'S HORSE

He collects light like a blade, sharpens it
night by night until a single flash
turns bone to paper,
skin to stone.

I am told not to look so I stand with my eyes
closed, turning my back on the sun.
They hose me down when he leaves
because his radiance makes me glow.

★

In the darkest hours he rides me bareback.
He has taught me to walk like a crane—
stately, elevated. Dew breaks under us.
He bows my neck against the rush of air.

He does not speak, bending his ear
to the wind in the redwoods, and when dawn
begins to shine through skin
we ride into the flames, blinded by reflections.

★

After the defeat his uniform is sent to a museum,
every crease preserved under glass.
He takes to wearing mufti: shapeless
suits that make him look

smaller, softer—a dead pet
waiting for the dignity of rigor mortis.

WILLING SUSPENSION

Konstantinbasilika, Trier

We could fight for days about what holds it up,
Christian faith or Roman engineering:
two centuries older than Hagia Sofia, vast
as a turbine hall though by some miracle
completely self-supporting. Bombed
during World War II, the roof and walls collapsed
in flames and while the fire-storm roared
the locals swore, swore on their dead children
that they heard the organ play, a ghostly requiem
soaring through the brimstone like a sign.
No mystery there: air trapped inside the pipes
was suddenly released, a final exhalation.
And yet the science doesn't change the fact
that this immense, improbable space dreamed up
by Constantine who learned to listen
to the voice of God, has both of us believing.

FREITOD

The Suicide of Paul Celan, 20th April 1970

Rise up against suicide and its instruments,
against ropes, blades, gas, guns, poison, pills,
against pens that claim you died *freiwillig,*
as though your final slip between the worlds of air
and water were somehow voluntary or optional—
a service charge at the foot of your bill.

If death were free, then this would be the tip
of a prolonged submersion in that trail of tears
where you had never learned to swim.

Pollarding the Limes

They arrive without warning, long before you've noticed
anything needs attention—two men in a black van
as seriously breezy with their ropes and power-saws
as the yellow leaf-shredder sizing up the limes.
Everything goes in: greenstick limbs, leaves
flopping like puppies' ears round the trunks,
whole branches lopped off and milled into chips,
a bosky compost to tart up the municipal borders.

For days you'll think of nothing else—those poor trees
splintered between sky and kerb, bending over backwards
to hold on. Then, sooner or later, going inside,
closing the door, you'll struggle to remember
how your landscape changed: the grim striptease,
the bitter requiem of falling timber.

Fall

Imagine the fall from grace,
the weight of the world on a bone,
comic-book humiliation—
the earth reeling you in feet
first, dark coils hissing
round your ankles, head
over heels and seeing stars.

It feels like the love of a vice.
What you remember is
the crack of logs, the chainsaw
scream of braking vowels
(*limber* to *lumber*, *run* to *rune*),
a wood-nymph's fingers
turning green then white.

What use are miracles—
articulation, balance,
Vorsprung durch Technik—
when each new step's
a leap in the dark
from which you wake breathless,
talking to your hand?

TIME AND MOTION

They said we should remove the pendulum.
Instead we wrapped the clock in sheets
and wedged it in a corner of the boot.
As we set off, the chimes began—the hour
and then the quarter hour, the half already
at its heels: a ghostly angelus that told us
it was later than we thought, the minutes
flashing by like white lines on the road.
Now we're ahead of ourselves, skidding
in the fast lane, screeching to a halt
within striking distance of home, opening
the doors, watching time run out
all over the hard shoulder.

NIGHTS ON THE UNDERGROUND

He's down here somewhere, sweating the city's heat.
He has a knack for it—sniffs me out through the maze of tunnels,
reels me in, hell for leather with his fake crucifix.

Sometimes he's gone for weeks. Sometimes the escalators
defeat him. He trips on the silliest of things,
limps after me, cursing: *Rattle her, rattle her like a dog.*

Later there'll be breath in my ear, a whiff of nicotine
and wormwood. See the busker in the next carriage—
that's him playing *Devil Doll* to the late-night crowd.

Don't ask for names, I'm down too deep. Rats run at his heels,
he shaves his beard in stages. When winter comes, he hoofs
along the tracks, warming my soul on the electric rail.

Red lights, infernal trains, a subterranean wind:
he'll haunt me till I find redemption, riding the live wire,
watching sparks fly at the end of the line.

DOPPELGÄNGER

Years later we bumped into each other,
eight months pregnant on a train to Scotland.
No getting around us, bellies wedged
across the corridor like freak-show sacs
galvanised by locomotive powers.
Was this real? It had the bladder-sting
of truth—locked eyes, deep-tissue fibrillation,
the struggle not to laugh or cry in case of leaks—
and for a few heavenly moments

everything came together:
our figure-hugging pose, the flashing sun,
the count-down of sleepers and signposts,
rattling mnemonics *taking us back,*
taking us back to a siding in the past
when we couldn't have imagined anything less
than this—our flesh and blood connecting
on the same celestial longitude,
live frogs jolting us from track to track.

MONA LISA'S EYEBROWS

Did he shave them himself, his blade
skating cack-handed across
her forehead until the bone broke
surface, china-smooth, jutting
like a prow above the veiled eyes,
the skin's eloquent *sfumato*?

Who knows what colour they were
or how they shaped her gaze;
whether they arched or beetled,
knitted or furrowed or met
in the middle, time-lapsing
like the werewolf's at full moon.

Brushed from the final picture
with a glaze that celebrates
the skull's mortal geometry,
they frown on bald conjecture—
inflections of a lost exchange
that raised an artless smile.

HOW TO BEHAVE OUT OF DOORS
The execution of Mata Hari, October 1917

The barracks at Vincennes, cold
even for October. No sun, a gruelly rain
> *Walk straight to the spot*
A clearing, one tree stripped bare,
a mound of earth to take stray bullets
> *If you should meet*
> *a gentleman of your acquaintance*
> *it is your privilege to bow*
The troops drawn up already,
twelve Zouaves, rifles at ease
> *Incline your feet more inward*
> *than outward*
Moist ground, heels sinking in
> *Keep your head steady*
> *arms by your sides, your countenance*
> *elevated*
No stake, no coward's blindfold
> *Do not run*
> *unless great occasion require it*
> *lest in such violent motions*
> *you fall*
Each man stares down his barrel
at her breast
> *Shun the exaggeration of trailing*
> *skirts and inappropriate hats*
The volley rings out, a puff
of greenish smoke
> *No loud tones, no*
> *boisterous laughter*
She settles to her knees, slips back
slowly, legs doubled up, face turned
towards the sky

It is not your aim to attract
the eye of the crowd but to escape
its notice

In her behaviour out of doors
the gentlewoman is quiet
and unassuming

Do not wave your arms about
as if you were flying

She knows how to die

WALL

All evening there were rumblings: my father
sweating in black tie, my mother snared
in a cocktail frock that swished like a fan.
Even the garden ants were playing up,
pouring from cracks in the lawn
with rustling wings pinned to their metal backs.

I put on my new petticoat and climbed
over our fence into the wood. A bristling
of needles, the chill of pine; arrows carved
in the bark, leaking a sour grey sap.
I knew I must follow the signs or be bundled
into the oven, eaten by witches, trapped

forever in the fairy-tale. But it was hard to keep
my head while night-owls thrummed like tanks
and waves of thunder boomed through the dark
like guns. My feet were numb, my hem was ripped,
the bread behind me on the path blew away
where it fell, a gust of silver crumbs.

We woke next day to road blocks and barbed wire,
a twitching of commentators and politicians.
No one had planned to build a wall, they said,
though it was obvious to any child
that wolves had turned at dawn into Alsatians,
masking their snarls and growls with doggy smiles.

THE FIRST EGG

Not a feather in sight—yet here it is, a glob
of spit or spunk to go to work on:
protein-rich salvation, sunrise in a shell.

The scribe cross-legged with his roll of papyrus
swears he's been goosed—that hot wind flapping
round his neck, that wild hissing from the wadi.

He aches as if he's squeezed out
alabaster rocks. Cracking the egg,
he draws the sign for God.

OLD SALT

In Memory of Tony Troup

At the end of a hotel breakfast overlooking the Cam
you lean across to tell me your story about
joining the Navy. I've heard it before—the piping
prep-school boy, the board of sea-dogs barking questions:
Why d'you want to join?
                    I don't.
                              Why not?
                                    Because my father says
you have to drink salt-water. You'd tried it once,
creeping down to the beach at Southsea to fill your hands,
your throat kippered raw, your tongue pickling to an eel
as you took it in, like the rod soaked in brine
before a birching. Their laughter couldn't cure you,
no more than gagging or puking. Yet here you are,
seventy years on, still going back, still
combing the slips of shingle for that small boy
frosted like a salt lick on the shore.

WOOD-BURNING STOVE

They wanted us to have it—their Norwegian stove recycled
from railway iron and scrap engines, a fire-proof gingerbread-
        house
that had roared heat from its belly for over thirty years:
easy to get spare parts, plenty of logs to keep us warm forever.

It was smaller out of its nook, the bricks behind it scorched
into a secret shadow-pelt that wouldn't rub off.
When we lifted it into the car, the door flew open, distressing
the garage floor with a last spill of ash from the flue—
ash that now was cold but perhaps remembered
the lovely leap of flames, the green heart of the timber.

Dry

When I came to the river
it was gone, the shock of water
drawn off, tapped to the lees
as if the sea had suddenly

swallowed its own spit, broken
with the past, given up on
bridges, weirs, the narrowness
of small-town bankability.

Ducks huddled and flapped.
Children stared in silence
at landlocked boats, at plastic bags
swanning in mud.

There was something unseemly
about it: the bed exposed
like the roof of a mouth,
ridged and wet, obscenely

intimate, a squalid by-way
shoaled with bricks and bottles,
bikes, prams, chains, tyres,
supermarket trolleys—

suspended, fossilized,
as if some vast conveyor belt
had ground to a halt mid-stream
and we were left to make do

with memories: a tang
of salt, a chime of sunlight
on broken glass, the gravel's
haunting sheen.

MOTORWAY BRIDGE

This green bridge spanning the twisted scar of the road
is a trick of the mind, an image
of primeval forest, Elysian fields, a sigh for higher
moral ground. Angelic flyover, perhaps?
—rather, a walkway from judgement hall
to execution place, lashed across the void
like something out of *Indiana Jones*.
A feat of engineering, man-made but natural,
wearing its leaves and umbrage like Great Birnam Wood;
a viaduct for deer, mice, ants, the shy hedgehog, the blind mole,
for all the animals that creep and crawl but have no wings,
so they can cross, and cross again,
deluded into thinking their fragmented space
is one big happy joined-up world
whose heavy metal roar is just a background noise
we're all immune to now, even that curious roebuck parting
the leaves to watch the dragons smoking down below.

Caged Elephants

There were things no one told us—
how dusk trickled slowly through the cracks
like something you could touch with your trunk,

a soft mist scented with myrtle and laurel,
voluptuous, weighed down by the rills
of brown birds tearing their throats, and pain

below the range of human hearing: the grief
of solitary, creamy moths, the terrified
crumbling of cement. Or how, beyond

watering distance, eyes would kipper in their sockets
and to weep would be like the first gasp
of a fresh wound, cruel and beautiful. How day

would no longer be that sweet climb
into brilliance—the sun oiling the warm
bark of the baobab tree, the horizon glittering

like a needle. How our ears would soon forget
the shape and weave of a continent,
which no amount of trumpeting could bring back

because we were stretched to the very limits
of illumination, our only constant,
fear—not fear of death or darkness or hunger

but the fear that we might go on hoping
for something better than this: a small
adjustment, or a giving in.

THIRST AND SLAKE

End of summer: the earth crackling like bark,
every layer peeled back, keening for rain.

How long it goes on—this see-saw
of dust and water, thirst and slake;
the leafing and unleafing of the trees.

No wind tonight. The moths hang
in the dark like flowers waiting to drop.

What pleasure to feel the whisper
of the mosquito!—his sly harpoon,
the itch of blood and hide, the flooding
of proteins and saliva; to know there will be
nights like this—rich-scented, wanton
with favours; the rustle of limbs
before the rains begin.

MULBERRY
for Cordelia

Because it's hard to talk of death, we talk about
the mulberry tree: its stooping trunk and delicate
fruit, the tooth-edged leaves that keep their grip
on stalk and branch through storm and stress
then on a quiet morning suddenly drop,
an orchestrated fall that takes an hour or two
to cast a mirror-image on the grass.

It waits through winter until every breath of frost
has passed, so drab you'll think it's dead.
When all the other trees have long since dressed
for spring, you'll wake from splintered dreams
one starless night to hear its leaf-buds
opening with such force they might be
God's green fingers snapping in the dark.

CEREBRAL ANEURYSM
The death of Elizabeth Bishop, October 1979

She would have enjoyed its definition
in the OED—not the thirteen-volume edition
she finally bought herself in Princeton,
collecting a degree the June
before she died, but in the one I own

in which the text is reproduced
micrographically so it has to be used
with a magnifying glass placed
over blocks of print that have been squeezed
onto the page and then reduced.

She might have recalled from Greek
classes at Vassar that what struck
her dumb at six o'clock
that Saturday after a terrible week
of illness, loneliness, and cancelled work

was rooted in the verb 'to widen out'
and came to mean ballooning of an artery
(in her case, in the brain), a sudden short
caused by disorders in the vascular coat,
unusual enough to merit a footnote

in any account of her life.
When she was found at Lewis Wharf
dead in the study, the phone was off
the hook, as if—or almost as if—
she'd tried to call from the afterlife

to specify what she could see and hear:
the view through virgin mirror
of that unmapped shore—
birds, fish, shadows, shallows, the roar
of something *cold dark deep and absolutely clear.*

INFANTA

The Infanta María Teresa poses for Diego Velázquez

THAT GIRL

You glance at me—then your black eyes
fall away to that girl on the canvas.

I might be a melon or a dead fish—
you need my bones to touch her in

but save your scumbles for her,
daubing and rubbing so she flushes into life.

You load your brush until it floods—
umber, red lake, smalt—

laying it on with small flicked strokes,
with slashing downward strokes,

dragging the colour across the weave,
letting it pool within the brushwork.

See how she rises to the task!—
how your wand enhances her contours,

glossing her shy lips,
ripening her cheeks like apples in the sun.

Oh, be gentle with her—you have her
in the palm of your hand

and bring her out so artfully
she might mistake you for a suitor.

WIG

Let me show you my hair,
how soft and pale it is under this wire,
how well it compliments my skin.

I do not think your brush can do it justice.
Can the wind catch thistledown?
Can yellow paint give us the sun?

BALTASAR CARLOS

Did they tell you?—my brother's dead—
sixteen years old, a military campaign in Zaragoza.

I try to picture it: the flash of swords, blood spurting
from a wound, his poor horse bolting back to the stable.

You like a challenge—couldn't you paint it for me?
He sat to you often, you know the colour of his skin,

the way the gorget ate into the soft flesh of his throat,
the way the red sash brought out

his tender lips, the bunny-pink of his eyes.
No need, this time, to emphasise his mastery

of the reins of power. Work up his costume
with your trademark strokes,

but save your sable brushes for the sky—
the pall of clouds, the black smoke rising from the cannons.

BUTTERFLIES

Last night they came alive,
shivering their silver threads like ghosts,
tasting the dark with their wings.

I tried to shake them off,
rolling from side to side against the bolster
until their abdomens crunched like shells,

but they were caught in the net
of my hair, laced to my skull
with brushwork strands

that crushed their bodies into pigment.
Couldn't you hear me screaming,
tearing my hair out by the roots?

Now I order you to paint them out—
to turn them into pretty ribbons,
slices of candied lemon, miniature fans.

Rear View

Who started this craze
for skirts as wide as a house?

I could give quarter
to a sound of pigs under these petticoats,

fill my bellied hoops
with geese and gourds fit for a banquet.

You've seen me in full sail,
listing along the corridors of power,

clipping the dwarfs' ears,
cutting the *meninas* down to size.

I beg you—salvage my reputation
with your brush,

trim my riggings,
scuttle the poisonous whispers

that you've stitched the canvas
to accommodate my arse.

INBRED

You claim it's easier to mix their blood
than size a second canvas—
all it takes is a splash of paint
and down my father goes.

When his jaw breaks surface,
jutting through the pigments
like a threat, you stick it back
with glue and manganese

then hold him under
while you slap her in, flushing
his manhood with your knife.
A lick of calcite shuts him up for good.

She rises from his shadow like a swan—
wife, queen, niece, twin—
a miracle of transubstantiation,
the very picture of the King.

I peer over your shoulder
and it's like opening a vein:
the Habsburg bloodline floods
her luminous skin, corrupts

the smoothness of the paint, smudges
her upper lip as if the past had power
to deform, and we were all
too close for comfort.

MARIANA'S LEGS

In one of the towns she visited
en route from Austria to Spain

the local artisans brought out their wedding gift—
a hundred pairs of stockings.

The Chamberlain sent them back:
A Spanish Queen does not have legs, he said.

Since then she has learnt to turn everything
down—her girlish laugh, her hems,

her Habsburg mouth—trusting in gravity
to keep her feet on the ground.

STEPMOTHER

Why must I stand like *her*?—
the same silly pose:
a fistful of lace, ribbons
at my wrist, my arms stuck out
like poles, my skirt as bulbous
as a Moorish dome.

At court they mix us up
like muffs
though any mole can see
we're as different
as eggs and chestnuts.
Look at that bumpy nose,
those sulky lips, that pothole
in the rough impasto of her chin—
I will not be her spit!

You're the one
who gives me to the world—
forget the pretty picture,
dress me as a child, a dwarf,
a servant gutting fish,
a *pícaro* with a pumpkin.
Bring out these bulging
rabbit eyes
so I can see myself.

If I must wear *her* wig,
when I am finished
we will both be dogs.

GUARDAINFANTE

You've chained me to this rock
with pearls, fisted my breath
with frills of pink tulle
so I am stiff as a doll,
hooped and farthingaled,

hostage to fashion
and privilege.
No one can touch me now,
chaste as a knife-edge
in my armoured cage.

BLUSH

They erupt like the pox,
daubs of vermilion bursting
through the desert of my dress,
blooming round my waist and wrists,
my shoulders, throat, and breast,
blushing to a feverish rouge
across my cheeks and hair.

I think of roses dropped
in snow, *patatas bravas*,
—or the blood I found
this morning on my linen,
a trail of dots and dashes
which I traced back with my fingers
to the wound your brush had drawn
between my legs,
flushing out all my secrets.

Zwey Kleine Uhrl

See these two little watches
dangling from my waist—
they've tied them here
so I can watch time fly
to the grave
on wings of scarlet ribbon.

MORTAL SIN

Have you heard the scandal
bruited in the corridors?
Even the dwarfs are taking the piss:
Nicolas Pertusato moons at me
in his doll's britches, Maribárbola
sniggers and twitches her *cuisses*.

They say—they all say—
you're painting me nude.
And I defend you—*no, no*—
are you blind? Look—
I'm wearing my wig, my crinoline,
my ornaments, my pearls,
my collar of pleated tulle, only
my face and hands are visible,
my throat, my wrists.

And then I watch you
load your coarsest brush
with russet, rose, and cream,
ivory, alabaster, buff.

LAS MENINAS

I don't understand why you need such a huge
canvas for a small princess—
my sister's five years old, too young to know
what it means to be turned into paint
(when just to look at her will be to taste her skin
on your brush, her sweet hair on your tongue).

I know your tricks: dissolving shadows,
light coming in through an open door,
the eloquent hands, the blurred reflections,
your palette rigged to create the illusion
of a moment frozen in time.

What you've forgotten is that life's a dream
no more real than my sister's smile
or the drink still slopping in her cup
which she will never be able to sip
however long she stands there in your frame.

THE PROPER VIEWING DISTANCE

Close up, your portraits
are a mess—a fury
of brown washes, storms of paint,
unblended brushstrokes,
dabs and flecks that could be
flowers, fireworks, flocks of birds,
small explosions signifying
nothing.

You tell me there's a proper viewing distance
where the fragments come together,
glimmers fusing into truth
as you withdraw your gaze.

Tear me to pieces—
break up my hands
                    my head
                        my heart—

Show me where we stand.

On the Market

You rub my flesh
until it glows, hatch
my wigs and crinolines
with a dry brush
and a warm glaze,
lay me out
under an awning
like a pomegranate
or a loaf of bread,
theirs for the taking—

Melon ready to split!

Now I am bought
by France,
they eat me
with their eyes

and I must stand
and watch them
lick the juice
from their fingers.

ISLA DE LOS FAISANES

Look at you, tricked out
in your fine black suit,
flashing your jewels
like a popinjay.

Hard to believe
you'd scrub up so well—
no drips on your doublet,
no turps or oil
to sour the breath
of all these lords and ladies
flocking for the ceremonies.

On this Isle of Pheasants
my future husband
is the king of cocks

but when I dream,
I dream of you:
your gaudy hands,
your ruthless gaze,
your loaded brush poised
over my canvas.

WEDDING DRESS

They say I steam
like a horse, that I am
toute en eau
under my gown.

It isn't sweat—
it's just my body
weeping tears.

GARLIC AND MOTHBALLS

Oh save me from these French who mince about
with noses in the air, as if I'm something they've found
on their shoes! They swear my breath stinks
of garlic, my Spanish dresses reek of mothballs.
They hate my dwarfs, my little dogs, my maids.
They ridicule my accent and my wigs,
claim that my liking for chocolate will stain
my front teeth black. It's all your fault—
your portraits flattered me with fairytales
of bee-stung lips, a waist like an egg-timer,
luminous eyes, skin the colour of frost.
You ground up azurite and lapis lazuli,
then dreamed up sleights of hand to take France in.
Now you must make her take to me.

DEAD

They tell me—No, I cannot take it in.
They tell me you are dead.
No. Dead of a fever in Madrid—
worn out by duties at my wedding—

stomach pains—exhaustion—
No. No. I see you blowing kisses
like a carp behind the tapestries
in the Spanish pavilion,

flashing your rapier
at the herds of courtiers
sniggering at my white skin,
my billowing crinoline.

You made me your masterpiece,
turned me on with your brush
till I fizzed and flushed
like a *feu d'artifice*.

Now who will light me up?
Mignard? Laumosnier? Beaubrun?
Piss-artists all of them, charlatans
who'd rather paint a cold fish than a ripe

peach. How can you be so cruel?
It's a mistake—
a prank to make me summon you back
with your palette and easel.

I will not cry. I will not be sad.
No. You are not dead.
The Queen of France will not
consent to it.

GRAVE GOODS

I watch my husband minting bastards
while one by one my babies die.

How I long for you to draw them back to life,
to stroke their foreheads with your softest brush,

bring out shawls to keep them warm,
playthings to amuse them in the grave—

rattles that chafe my ears, apples
so plump and smooth I lean to take a bite.

BLIND EYE

a queen does not need to be
heard
a queen does not need to be
told
a queen does not need to be
loved

a queen needs water under her window
a queen needs dogs prayers nuns chocolate
a queen needs to turn a blind eye
a queen needs smooth handling, thinly applied washes
       small, flicked strokes
         a sable brush
         the miraculous facility of paint

NOTES

The Infanta María Teresa was born in 1638, daughter of Philip IV of Spain and his first wife Isabella of Bourbon. The demand for portraits of the young Infanta once she reached marriageable age coincided with the return from Italy of the court painter, Velázquez.

Baltasar Carlos: son of Philip IV and Isabella of Bourbon, brother of María Teresa, and heir to the Spanish throne. Velázquez painted him several times. His premature death in 1646 at the age of sixteen while on a military campaign with Philip in Zaragoza was the beginning of a crisis for the Spanish dynasty.

Butterflies: Fragment of a lost, possibly half-length portrait of the Infanta María Teresa, painted by Velázquez in 1652/3. Her wig is decorated with starched ribbons in the shape of butterflies.

Rear View: The dimensions of Velázquez' full-length portrait of Philip's second wife, Mariana of Austria, were enlarged by stitching a band of cloth along the left side of the canvas, probably to fit in the queen's large costume (see *Velázquez: The Technique of Genius* by Jonathan Brown and Carmen Garrido, Yale University Press, 1998).

Inbred: Radiography and infrared reflectography have shown that, in his 1652 portrait of Mariana, Velázquez painted the head of the queen over an unfinished portrait of the king. Mariana was Philip's niece and they shared many of the Habsburg traits. The sole surviving heir of their marriage, Carlos Segundo, was sickly, retarded and impotent: his jaw was so deformed by mandibular prognathism (Habsburg jaw or Austrian lip) that he was unable to chew.

Mariana's Legs/Stepmother: The Infanta María Teresa's stepmother, Mariana, was also her cousin and only four years older than her. The similarity of their Habsburg features has caused frequent confusion when identifying portraits of them by Velázquez.

Guardainfante: Crinoline.

Zwey Kleine Uhrl: Two little watches (described thus in the inventory of Archduke Leopold William's collection which included a full-length portrait of the Infanta María Teresa).

Mortal Sin: The painting of nudes for public display was considered 'pecado mortal' (mortal sin) and could be punished by excommunication and exile.

Nicolas Pertusato and **Maribárbola** were two of the dwarfs in the Royal Household.

Las Meninas: Portrait of the Infanta Margarita in *Las Meninas*, painted by Velázquez in 1656. Margarita was María Teresa's half-sister, the first child of Philip IV's second marriage to his niece, Mariana.

l. 12 **life's a dream:** *La vida es Sueño*, a play by Pedro Calderón de la Barca, published in 1636.

Isla de los Faisanes: A fluvial island in the Bidassoa river in the Pyrenees, under joint sovereignty of France and Spain, this was the setting for the signing of a peace treaty between the two countries which paved the way for María Teresa's wedding to Louis XIV of France in June 1660. Velázquez had been appointed Chamberlain of the Royal Palace (*aposentador mayor*) in 1652, a post which would involve him in the planning and staging of the historic events on the island. He was responsible for decorating the Spanish side of the pavilion for the occasion and is said to have participated in the wedding ceremony wearing jewels over a black suit trimmed with silverpoint lace.

Wedding dress: Official pamphlets describing the event for the French reading public noted that by mid-afternoon on the day of the wedding, the Queen was dripping with sweat and was obliged to retire to her room.

Dead: On June 26th 1660, Velázquez returned to Madrid after the wedding ceremonies. He wrote: *I have returned to Madrid, worn out by journeying all night and working all day.* On July 31st he was overcome by pains in the stomach and the heart, and he died a few days later, on August 6th.

Grave Goods: María Teresa gave birth to six children, three boys and three girls, all of whom died in childhood, apart from Louis, *Le Grand Dauphin*. The King, meanwhile, had a succession of mistresses and several illegitimate children.

Acknowledgements

Grateful acknowledgement is made to the editors of the following publications, in which these poems, or earlier versions of them, have appeared or are due to appear:

Ambit: 'Black Pudding', 'Doppelgänger'; *Equinox*: 'Mona Lisa's Eyebrows'; Limelight: 'Faun', 'Floe', 'Knowledge', 'Motorway Bridge'; *Modern Poetry in Translation*: 'Snow in April'; *Mslexia*: 'Sixpences'; *PN Review*: 'On the Rocks', 'Wood-burning Stove'; *Poetry London*: 'The Penance of St John Chrysostom'; *Poetry Review*: 'About Suffering'; *Poetry Wales*: 'Beginnings', 'That Girl'; *Smiths Knoll*: 'Mariana's Legs'; *Stand*: 'Fall', 'Pollarding the Limes', 'Mortal Sin'; *The Frogmore Papers*: 'Dry', 'Nights on the Underground'; *The London Magazine*: 'Wall'; *The Warwick Review*: 'Detachment'.

'The Final Stretch' won 1st prize in Poetry on the Lake 2003. 'Country Living' won 2nd prize in the 2006 Arvon International Poetry Competition. 'Nox Elephantorum' won 3rd prize in the 2005 Keats-Shelley Memorial Prize. 'Caged Elephants' was commended in the 2005 Myeloma Poetry Competition. 'Old Salt' was commended in the 2006 Tonbridge Poetry Competition. 'Harvesting' and 'Thirst and Slake' were commended in the 2005 Ware Poetry Competition.

Warmest thanks go to Rosie Allen, Claire Crowther, Barbara Daniels, Lorraine Mariner, Naomi May and Stephanie Williams for their on-going inspiration and encouragement.

Printed in the United Kingdom by
Lightning Source UK Ltd., Milton Keynes
137117UK00001B/235-294/P